DISCARD

THE PACIFIC OCEAN

BY JUNIATA ROGERS

ASIA

NORTH AMERICA

PACIFIC OCEAN

SOUTH AMERICA

AUSTRALIA

Published by The Child's World®
1980 Lookout Drive • Mankato, MN 56003-1705
800-599-READ • www.childsworld.com

Credits: APHITHANA/Shutterstock.com: 13; Courtney Wise/Shutterstock.
com: 18; Creative icon styles: 5, 14 (compass); Hills Outdoors/Shutterstock.
com: 6; Kelly Headrick/Shutterstock.com: 10; NOAA/NOAA.gov: 17; pr2is/
Shutterstock.com: cover, 1; Rich Carey/Shutterstock.com: 9, 21

ISBN HARDCOVER: 9781503825048
ISBN PAPERBACK: 9781622434367
LCCN: 2017960230

Printed in the United States of America
PA02373

TABLE OF CONTENTS

WHERE IN THE WORLD?

Where is the Pacific Ocean? Look at the map. Do you see North and South America? They are to the east. Now find Asia. Australia is below it. They are to the west. The Pacific Ocean is in the middle.

Fifty-five countries have borders along the Pacific Ocean.

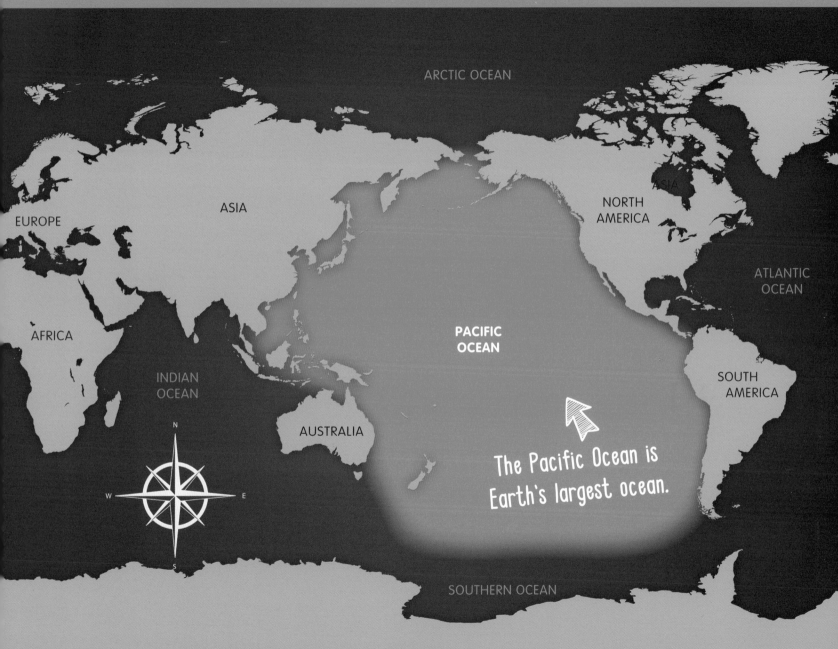

ARCTIC OCEAN

EUROPE

ASIA

ASIA

NORTH
AMERICA

ATLANTIC
OCEAN

AFRICA

PACIFIC
OCEAN

INDIAN
OCEAN

SOUTH
AMERICA

AUSTRALIA

The Pacific Ocean is
Earth's largest ocean.

SOUTHERN OCEAN

ANTARCTICA

The Pacific Ocean is bigger than all of Earth's land areas put together.

A BIG OCEAN

The world has five oceans. The Pacific Ocean is the biggest. It covers almost a third of the whole planet.

The Pacific Ocean covers more than 63 million square miles (163 million sq. km).

DEEP AND WIDE

The Pacific Ocean is big. It is also deep.

The **Challenger Deep** is in the Pacific

Ocean. It is the world's deepest place.

The Challenger Deep is seven miles
(11 km) deep. It is located
near the island of Guam.

The average depth of the Pacific Ocean is about 13,000 feet (4,000 m).

The explorer Ferdinand
Magellan named the
Pacific Ocean around 1521.

HOW'S THE WEATHER?

The word "pacific" means peaceful and calm. Some areas of the Pacific Ocean stay calm most of the time. Other parts get stormy.

El Niño and La Niña are times when the Pacific Ocean becomes warmer or cooler. Storms, flooding, and droughts can all be caused by El Niño and La Niña.

BIG STORMS

Typhoons are big storms. They form in the Pacific Ocean. They happen when warm and cool air mix together. Typhoons have strong winds. They can bring heavy rain and flooding.

In North America, typhoons are called hurricanes.

Typhoons bring winds with speeds of more than 74 mph (119 kmh)

About 90% of all earthquakes happen along the Ring of Fire.

RING OF FIRE

The **Ring of Fire** is a lively place. Many volcanoes are here. Earthquakes often shake things up. Earth's surface is changing here. Volcanoes slowly rise from the sea.

More than 75% of the world's volcanoes are in the Ring of Fire.

The Great Barrier Reef is home to thousands of different kinds of fish and animals.

WONDERFUL HOME

The Pacific Ocean holds many wonders.

The **Great Barrier Reef** is one. This reef is found just off Australia's coast. Many animals live here. The reef looks like rock. It is not. It is made of **coral**.

The Great Barrier Reef can be seen from space.

MORE TO LEARN

We are still learning about the Pacific Ocean. Who knows what we will learn next? What do you hope we will find?

Most of the world's islands are found in the Pacific Ocean.

The Pacific Ocean is more than 15 times the size of the United States.

GLOSSARY

black smoker (BLAK SMOH-ker): A black smoker is a vent on the ocean floor where very hot jets of water escape.

Challenger Deep (CHAL-eng-jer DEEP): The Challenger Deep is the deepest place on Earth.

coral (KOR-ul): Coral is a rocklike material made from the skeletons of tiny animals called coral polyps (pah-lips).

Great Barrier Reef (GRAYT BARE-ee-er REEF): The Great Barrier Reef is the largest coral reef in the world. It is more than 1,400 miles (2,250 km) long.

Ring of Fire (RING of FIRE): The Ring of Fire is the area around the edge of the Pacific Ocean where there is a lot of volcanic activity.

typhoon (ty-FOON): A typhoon is a large, swirling storm. In North America, typhoons are called hurricanes.

TO FIND OUT MORE

Books

Oachs, Emily Rose. *Pacific Ocean*. Minneapolis, MN: Bellwether Media. 2016.

Spilsbury, Louise, and Richard Spilsbury. *Pacific Ocean*. Chicago, IL: Heinemann Raintree, 2015.

Wilsdon, Christina. *Ultimate Oceanpedia: The Most Complete Ocean Reference Ever*. Washington, DC: National Geographic Children's Books, 2016.

Woodward, John. *Ocean: A Visual Encyclopedia*. New York, NY: DK Publishing, 2015.

Web Sites

Visit our Web site for links about the Pacific Ocean:

childsworld.com/links

Note to Parents, Teachers, and Librarians: We routinely verify our Web links to make sure they are safe and active sites. So encourage your readers to check them out!

INDEX

ABOUT THE AUTHOR

Juniata Rogers grew up in Newport, RI, an island town on the Atlantic Ocean. She has worked as a naturalist, an art model, and a teacher. She's been writing professionally for 25 years, and currently lives near Washington, DC.